ALIEN
ABDUCTIONS

by Jenny Mason

STORY LIBRARY

MORE TO EXPLORE

www.12StoryLibrary.com

12-Story Library is an imprint of Bookstaves.

Developed and produced for 12-Story Library by Focus Strategic Communications Inc.

Library of Congress Cataloging-in-Publication Data
Names: Mason, Jenny (Children's author), author.
Title: Alien abductions / by Jenny Mason.
Description: Mankato : 12-Story Library, 2022. | Series: Aliens! |
Includes bibliographical references and index. | Audience: Ages 10–12 | Audience: Grades 4–6
Identifiers: LCCN 2020012968 (print) | LCCN 2020012969 (ebook) | ISBN 9781632359308 (library binding) |
ISBN 9781632359650 (paperback) | ISBN 9781645820963 (pdf)
Subjects: LCSH: Alien abduction—Juvenile literature. | Human-alien encounters—Juvenile literature
Classification: LCC BF2050 .M358 2022 (print) | LCC BF2050 (ebook) | DDC 001.942—dc23
LC record available at https://lccn.loc.gov/2020012968
LC ebook record available at https://lccn.loc.gov/2020012969

Photographs ©: ktsdesign/Shutterstock.com, cover, 1; IgorZh/Shutterstock.com, 4; rtuckertow/YouTube.com, 5; ktsdesign/Shutterstock.com, 5; adike/Shutterstock.com, 6; Ivan Bilibin/PD, 7; Vera Petruk/Shutterstock.com, 7; helena.40proof/CC2.0, 7; Sasa Kadrijevic/Shutterstock.com, 8; Fer Gregory/Shutterstock.com, 8; Monique/YouTube.com, 9; Library of Congress, 9; XX, 10; Becket01/CC4.0, 10; solarseven/Shutterstock.com, 11; Chancey2001/YouTube.com, 11; 3D generator/Shutterstock.com, 12; Melkor3D/Shutterstock.com, 13; GrandeDuc/Shutterstock.com, 13; Linda Bucklin/Shutterstock.com, 14; Blackdog1966/Shutterstock.com, 14; Swansea UFO Network/YouTube.com, 15; vijaifoon13/Shutterstock.com, 16; Digital Storm/Shutterstock.com, 16; Digital Storm/Shutterstock.com, 17; CrackerClips Stock Media/Shutterstock.com, 17; OpenMindsTV/YouTube.com, 18; David Leveson/Alamy, 18; Rawpixel/Shutterstock.com, 19; Ovni Languedoc/YouTube.com, 19; SMG2019/CC4.0, 20; lassedesignen/Shutterstock.com, 20; adike/Shutterstock.com, 21; Robert Sheaffer/CC3.0, 21; Tasnim News Agency/CC4.0, 22; Gorodenkoff/Shutterstock.com, 22; GrandeDuc/Shutterstock.com, 23; Mizkit/Shutterstock.com, 23; Gordonkoff/Shutterstock.com, 24; vchal/Shutterstock.com, 25; Sasa Kadrijevic/Shutterstock.com, 25; Troyrthayne/PD, 26; Carol Rainey/CC4.0, 27; PD, 27; Fer Gregory/Shutterstock.com, 28; Professor Plasmid/YouTube.com, 29; Best UFO Sighting/YouTube.com, 29

About the Cover

Did a flying saucer abduct this man and his car?

Access free, up-to-date content on this topic plus a full digital version of this book. Scan the QR code on page 31 or use your school's login at 12StoryLibrary.com.

Table of Contents

Carried Away: Betty and Barney Hill

Betty and Barney Hill were headed home. It was late at night on September 19, 1961. They saw unidentified lights in the sky. They arrived home. They could not remember three hours of the journey. Ten days later, nightmares rattled Betty.

4

UFO detectives questioned the Hills.

Later, a psychiatrist hypnotized them. Under hypnosis, the Hills' story grew. A flying orb chased their car. Little, human-like men captured them. On a spaceship, they had medical exams. Betty even chatted with the alien leader. Weirdly, their aliens were identical to those on a popular TV show.

The Hills were big news for two reasons. One: it was the first alien abduction in the US. Two: they were a biracial couple. For decades, most abduction stories matched the Hills' account.

4:00

The predawn hour when aliens almost abducted the Knowles family

- January 20, 1988: The family was driving through Western Australia.
- An egg-like ship lifted the car briefly. It dropped the car and flew away.
- After the Hills' abduction, aliens often targeted late-night drivers.

5

Attention Grabbers: The First Aliens

A mysterious creature appears. It snatches a person. The victim is held captive in a strange place. Eventually, the victim returns home. Those details summarize a basic alien abduction story. They also apply to many ancient stories across human history.

Scholars call these stories mythical patterns. Myths are stories told repeatedly over a long time. The patterns make them common worldwide. That is why so many cultures have Cinderella stories and vampire tales. As societies change, the characters also change.

Fairies. Leprechauns. The bunyip. Strix. Baba Yaga. The witch in a gingerbread house. All of these characters are people thieves. Many are

Baba Yaga (left) and a leprechaun (right).

short and human-like. Over time, these figures became aliens. Some of them glow or become balls of light. Aliens often use blinding lights. Time changed magic powers into magical technology. The magical world in myths became the spaceship.

The Cottingley Fairies were faked by two British girls. They admitted they used cardboard cutouts.

THINK ABOUT IT

Families can create myths. What personal stories does your family pass down?

44
Percent of British people who have seen a fairy

- The poll was conducted in 2018.
- Women see fairies more often than men do.
- In the US, men are more likely to report a UFO sighting.

A Lucky Ax-ident: Meng Zhaoguo

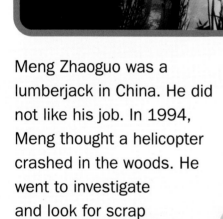

Meng Zhaoguo was a lumberjack in China. He did not like his job. In 1994, Meng thought a helicopter crashed in the woods. He went to investigate and look for scrap metal. Then something whacked Meng's head.

He woke up in his house. A few nights later, Meng floated out of bed. A 10-foot-(3-m) tall alien woman floated nearby. She had six fingers and braided fur.

A month later, Meng floated through the ceiling onto a spaceship. Speaking Chinese,

Meng claimed that he was abducted by a female alien.

1.4 billion
China's population in 2019

- Meng's was the first alien abduction reported in China. Meng passed a lie-detector test.
- Chinese UFO clubs claim thousands of members.
- Eight hundred people attended Hong Kong's first UFO Expo in 2019.

Hypnosis and a lie detector test proved that Meng Zhaoguo thought he was telling the truth.

aliens told him about their dying planet. After this incident, Meng found some luck. His story made him briefly famous. That fame helped him get a better job.

Isaac Asimov, circa 1959.

DOUBT IT

Scientists, writers, and magicians teamed up in 1976. They formed the Committee for Skeptical Inquiry (CSI). They use science to check alien cases. Isaac Asimov, a famous science fiction writer, was a CSI founder. So was astronomer Carl Sagan.

Reality Check: John Mack

During the 1990s, he interviewed hundreds of experiencers. This is what people who have contact with aliens are called. He even traveled to Zimbabwe, Africa. Over 60 children at a school there saw aliens and a UFO.

At first, Mack suspected that experiencers had mental illness. Over time, he changed his mind. Alien abduction

Imagine something scary happened to you. Everyone you told teased you. Or, they laughed and doubted you. This is a common experience among people abducted by aliens. Dr. John E. Mack treated abductees differently.

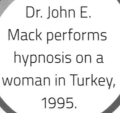

Dr. John E. Mack performs hypnosis on a woman in Turkey, 1995.

Mack was an award-winning psychiatrist. He helped children for many years. Then he began treating alien abductees.

10

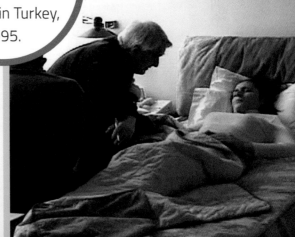

stories added new ways to see reality. Maybe humankind did not actually know what reality was. And above all, experiencers deserved kindness.

Their abductions were sometimes nightmares. Some critics said Mack was confirming delusions. They said that he harmed mentally ill people.

$19.95

Cost for alien abduction insurance, one-time payment

- About 6,000 people have purchased the insurance from a Florida company.
- The abducted person can receive $10 million. It pays out $1 per year for 10 million years.
- In the UK, 30,000 people got some out-of-this-world protection.

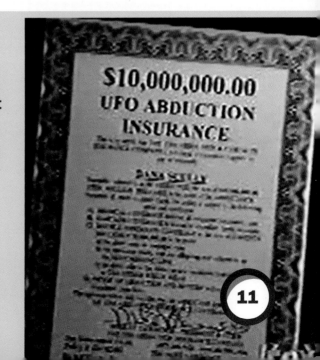

$10,000,000.00 UFO ABDUCTION INSURANCE

Ups and Downs: Abduction Statistics

A few years ago, many Americans believed in aliens. More than 75 percent thought aliens had visited Earth. That means three out of every four people shared the belief. Belief in alien abduction is also common.

At least one in 25 Americans believe they were abducted by aliens.

Beliefs are like mirrors. They can reflect world events. For instance, in the 1960s, hardly anyone reported UFOs as spaceships. But then, the first people landed on the moon in 1969. Three decades later, American beliefs had changed. Nearly half believed that UFOs came from outer space.

Illustration of aliens experimenting on a human.

Child abuse reports soared in the 1980s. After that, aliens snatched more children. Medical breakthroughs stormed the 1990s. Afterward, many victims' stories included surgical operations. More recently, alien abduction reports dropped. Why? Doctors understand the brain better. They see how it makes imagined experiences seem real.

96

Percent of Americans who knew about UFOs in a 1966 poll

- Fewer people knew Gerald Ford was the US President at the time.
- Alien contact and encounters were friendly before the 1960s.
- Aliens became dangerous as wars around the world got worse.

THINK ABOUT IT

What might be the next big event to shape our views on aliens?

Frequent Flyer: Hilary Porter

The first time it happened, Hilary Porter was 5. It was the early 1950s. She was playing outside her home in the UK. An alien with scaly skin appeared. He dragged Porter into a field. He shoved her into a disk-shaped ship.

Porter saw many electronics with colorful lights. The alien

Examinations by aliens are often reported by people who claim they were abducted.

Many years later, Porter still recalls the times she believed she was abducted.

examined her. She woke up in a field half a mile from home. Her mother found her.

Abductions have occurred throughout Porter's life. After each abduction, she returns injured and ill.

Porter knows people doubt her stories. They may also assume she is not very smart. Still, she has no control over the alien contact. It damages her well-being.

HOOKED

In 1976, four friends went night fishing on Maine's Allagash River. A large, glowing object chased their canoe. All four blacked out. They came to on shore. Twelve years later, their nightmares matched. Under hypnosis, one recalled their alien abduction on a spaceship.

109.1
Average IQ of an abduction experiencer

- An IQ test measures intelligence. Experiencers have higher IQs than other people.
- When tested, experiencers also show greater mental health.
- Research data suggests that stereotypes about experiencers are wrong.

7

Caught in a Tractor Beam: Antonio Villas Boas

The tractor died. Bad timing. Antonio Villas Boas needed a fast getaway.

The Brazilian farmer had waited for nightfall. Daytime was too hot for plowing. Boas saw a red star swoop near him. As it came closer, he realized it was a spaceship. It landed, and four human-like beings sprang out. Boas ditched the tractor. He ran away.

The aliens beamed Boas onto their ship.

The creatures captured Boas. They forced him onto the ship. They coated him in gel and took blood samples. Then they gave him a tour of the ship. He met a strange but beautiful alien woman. Boas was then returned to his farm.

Finding truth in Boas' story is difficult. By that time in 1957, many science fiction novels had described similar stories. Popular comic books did, too. Boas read these comics. Is it any wonder those stories crash-landed in people's imaginations?

1954
Year aliens in UFOs stories swept across Europe and South America

- Many people saw short, human-like beings in spacecraft.
- In Caracas, people saw hairy dwarfs.
- The dwarfs flew a ball-shaped ship, not a saucer.

Rescue Mission: CERO

Yvonne Smith worked as a therapist. She treated people who suffered intense fears. The condition is called trauma.

Very scary events cause trauma. Smith hypnotized her patients. Many revealed they had been abducted by aliens.

While they were abducted, time stopped. Little beings examined them. They took tissue samples. They took fluids from the body. The abduction experiencers had nowhere to go for help. No one believed them. Smith created the Close

Aliens examine a woman on their spacecraft.

Experiencers meet to discuss their abduction stories.

Encounters Research Organization (CERO) in 1992.

CERO helped experiencers. It invited them to meet and share stories. Many people felt relief. Their intense fear eased. CERO grew into an international organization.

700

Estimated number of alien abduction cases Smith treated over two decades

- Doctors, engineers, and military officials experienced abductions.
- Smith frequently appeared on TV to defend experiencers.
- The Discovery Channel. The History Channel. The Sci-Fi Channel. All interviewed Smith.

Myriame Belmyr (left), 2017

PROGRAMMED TO HELP

Myriame Belmyr was a French computer programmer. In 1987, aliens abducted her. She struggled to find help after the scary experience. In 2008, she formed a CERO group in France. The group brings experiencers together. It helps them heal.

Lost in the Woods: Travis Walton

The nighttime forest flooded with light. Travis Walton saw it. The six men with him in 1975 also saw it. They worked in the woods in Arizona. They were headed home.

The men supposed a plane crashed. Walton went to investigate. The bright light pulled him into a spaceship. The other men drove away

Travis Walton, 2019.

for help. The police questioned them over several days. Finally, Walton reappeared.

He claimed aliens had held him captive. The three creatures had bald heads and big eyes.

1993
Year the movie *Fire in the Sky* was released

- The film was adapted from Walton's book about his abduction.
- Before Walton, alien abduction reports were rare.
- Steven Spielberg's film *Close Encounters of the Third Kind* was a hit in 1977.

They conducted experiments on him. Walton's case seemed unique because he had so many witnesses. Later, investigators discovered it was a trick. Some witnesses were paid to lie.

THE ALIEN DETECTIVE

Philip J. Klass was a journalist and UFO detective. Many called him the "Sherlock Holmes" of alien research. He disproved many alien abduction claims. He found no evidence to support Travis Walton's story.

21

10

Checkmate: Alien Chess

Kirsan Ilyumzhinov, 2016.

Kirsan Ilyumzhinov loved chess. So much so that he built an entire chess-themed city. In 1997, Ilyumzhinov was the President of Kalmykia, Russia. On September 18 of that year, Ilyumzhinov said he was abducted by aliens.

He was napping. The doors to his balcony swung open. Aliens in yellow spacesuits took him to a giant spaceship. They flew Ilyumzhinov to a far-away star. They needed to pick up some tools there. They gave Ilyumzhinov oxygen. They also gave him a yellow suit.

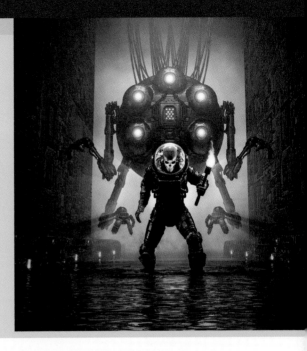

40

Number of witnesses who saw a UFO land in Voronezh, Russia

- On September 27, 1989, the ship landed in a park.
- A robotic creature came out of the ship.
- It paralyzed some witnesses. Others disappeared before the ship flew away.

The aliens told Ilyumzhinov about the universe. How it was full of intelligent life. They showed him around their ship. Back at the apartment, the president's assistants searched for him. They were shocked when he suddenly reappeared. Meeting aliens was a great honor for Ilyumzhinov because he believed they invented chess.

It is believed chess was invented in India about 1,500 years ago.

Probe-lem Solved: Recent Research

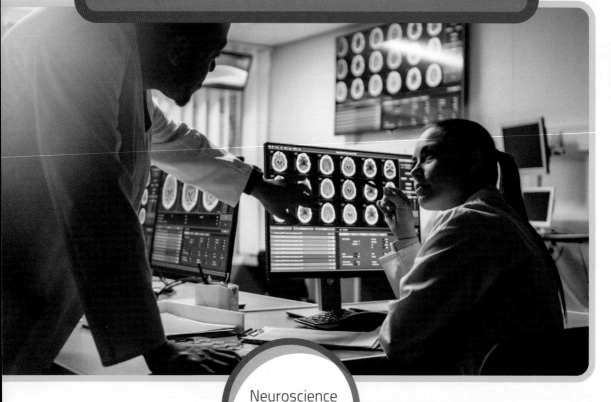

The many alien abduction reports make one thing clear. Experiencers go through a lot. They need help, not teasing.

Life in space has not yet been found. Investigators cannot find real evidence

Neuroscience is the study of the brain.

of aliens on Earth. So doctors are relying on neuroscience to help.

We now know a lot about the brain. For example, the brain has strange powers. It can create false smells and sounds. During sleep, different parts of the brain

Dreams of aliens can seem real.

turn on or off. As a result, a person can have sleep paralysis. Dreams and reality mix. Floating. Flashing lights. Prodding. Being trapped on an exam table. Experiencer stories match sleep paralysis symptoms.

THINK ABOUT IT

Have you ever had a dream feel like reality? What made it seem factual? Can you recall any sounds, smells, or tastes?

20

Percent of people who have experienced sleep paralysis

- Not enough sleep can cause "waking dreams." A waking dream is a dreamlike situation just before sleep.
- Signals can jam. The two brain halves detect a stranger lurking.
- Some people have woken up during surgery. Later, they think the doctors were aliens.

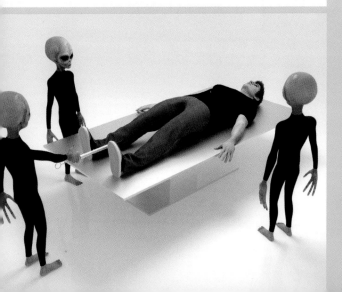

Seeing Is Believing: Elliot Budd Hopkins

Killer aliens were invading Earth. The news blasted from the radio in 1938. Budd Hopkins was little when he heard it.

The alien invasion news scared Hopkins and his family. It scared thousands of other listeners. Luckily, it was just a radio play. The story came from

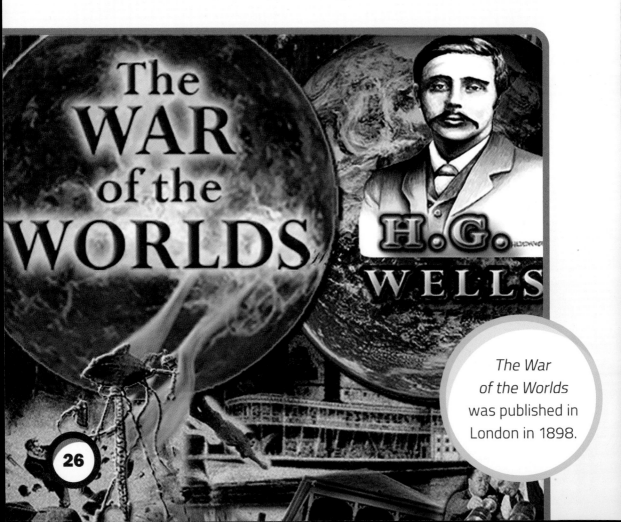

The War of the Worlds was published in London in 1898.

3,700,000

Number of Americans Hopkins estimated had been abducted

- He polled nearly 6,000 people in 1991.
- The results Hopkins calculated have been disputed.
- Some critics claim hypnosis creates false memories.

H.G. Wells's novel, *The War of the Worlds*. Still, the scary memory stayed with him.

Hopkins saw a UFO in the 1960s. Curious, he interviewed alien abduction experiencers. He became the first person to gather their stories. He also used hypnosis to help them remember details. Not surprisingly, Hopkins was certain aliens were a threat to humankind.

Whitley Strieber's book *Communion: A True Story* tells of his experience with his own alien abduction.

ALIEN HOLIDAY

In 1985, Whitley Strieber woke from a nap. He saw a shadowy figure. He then lost awareness. He woke in the woods. Strieber contacted Budd Hopkins, who suggested hypnosis. While hypnotized, Strieber recalled a painful abduction. Aliens stuck a needle in his brain. A doctor said Strieber had a brain condition that caused hallucinations.

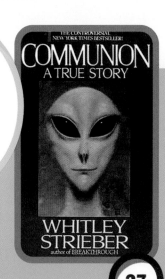

Above and Beyond

Party on Pluto:
Alien Abduction Day
March 20 is Alien Abduction Day. Celebrate with alien costumes, movies, or books. Visit the nearest space or UFO museum. No one knows when this event began. A Canadian toy company made it world-famous in 2008.

Welcome Home: Cosmic Door Mats

In 2017, the International Astronautical Congress used alien welcome mats. Special colors and shapes meant "welcome." Researchers analyzed the mats. They looked for signs of alien foot (or tentacle) traffic. No traces were found. Luckily, no one was abducted from the conference.

Going Green: Alien Climate Crusaders

Dr. Young-hae Chi knows what aliens want. They want to save Earth from climate change. The Oxford professor also believes aliens will stop nuclear disasters, too.

Glossary

biracial
Involving people from two races.

critic
A person who gives opinions or who disapproves of something.

delusion
A belief in the reality of something that is not real.

hallucination
An image, sound, or smell that seems real but does not exist.

hypnosis
A sleep-like state in which a person can hear and respond to questions or suggestions.

myth
A story repeated over time to explain a practice, belief, or natural occurrence.

neuroscience
The study of the structure and function of the brain.

paralyze
To make (someone or something) unable to function, act, or move.

psychiatrist
A doctor who treats mental or emotional disorders.

skeptic
A person who questions or doubts something.

stereotype
An often unfair and untrue belief about other people or things.

trauma
A very difficult or unpleasant experience that causes someone to have mental or emotional problems, usually for a long time.

Read More

Bowman, Chris. *Paranormal Mysteries. The Betty and Barney Hill Alien Abduction.* Hopkins, MN: Bellwether Media, 2019.

Chudler, Eric H. *Brain Lab for Kids: 52 Mind-Blowing Experiments, Models, and Activities to Explore Neuroscience.* Beverly, MA: Quarto Publishing, 2018.

Knight, Laura. *Kid Astronaut: Space Adventure.* Irvine, CA: Friendly Planet Club, 2018.

Owings, Lisa. *Investigating the Unexplained. Alien Abductions.* Hopkins, MN: Bellwether Media, 2018.

Visit 12StoryLibrary.com

Scan the code or use your school's login at **12StoryLibrary.com** for recent updates about this topic and a full digital version of this book. Enjoy free access to:

- Digital ebook
- Breaking news updates
- Live content feeds
- Videos, interactive maps, and graphics
- Additional web resources

Note to educators: Visit 12StoryLibrary.com/register to sign up for free premium website access. Enjoy live content plus a full digital version of every 12-Story Library book you own for every student at your school.

Index

About the Author

Jenny Mason has always lived in UFO country. She grew up a few hours from Roswell, New Mexico. She currently lives in Colorado near the UFO Highway. She will go anywhere in search of amazing stories.